Interstellar Thoughts

William Ennis

Copyright © 2019, by William Ennis
All rights reserved
ISBN: 9781081379155

I discovered a passion for writing poetry in late 2017, following a crash that made me question my entire life up to that point, and reshape my vision of the world and myself. I learned from this experience that pain and sorrow can somehow push people to accomplish beautiful things, and surpass themselves in their healing process. This was the case for me, through the poems that I have been writing these past few months.

Interstellar Thoughts is rooted in my desire as a young poet to reach the stars with words and rhymes, looking higher to better contemplate this void that makes us feel so small, but also looking down on myself to better understand my feelings. It is colored with blues and melancholy, as much as it is with hope and life, in the field of possibilities that is space.

These thoughts I call "interstellar" are dedicated to anyone aspiring to something greater, in a quest for wonder and fulfillment.

Thank you for reading my words.
It means so much to me.

William

So I set night
To the sky
To burn
With ink
And dreams
To bring light
To these thoughts
I call "interstellar"

Lost in between

Glowing heart

The glowing light
In your heart
Will be my soul guide
In the dark

For my drifting soul
Has lost its way
Among the shadows
Of yesterday

Mermaid

My heart is a sailor
Lost in troubled seas
Your mermaid voice
I follow within

Constellated notes
In obscure skies
Shades of heavenly echoes
Keep my soul beating

Seabed of your ocean

Awaking on
The seabed of your ocean
The only lights
From the surface
Here
Are from your soul
I see
Beams across dimensions
In a dream
I am
Wide awake

The eyes of dew

Lying on sunny grass
In dawn light
With the softest of piano notes
In the most moving sky

This is when I feel complete
This is when I remember
Your glowing eyes of dew

My compass

My vintage compass
Always points to your heart
Where my fears disappear
And become sparks

I shelter myself
From the glowing storm
'Cause the lightning within
You have always worn

Is it you

Is it the wind
Drifting
On the wings
Of a butterfly
Is it the sun
Burning for
Something new
Is it love
Crawling like
The missing waves
Of the open ocean

Inner stars

Show me how
To cut through
This night skin
Of mine

My inner stars
Want to escape
From the darkness
That keeps them
From shining
Out loud

Open sunlit road

Getting lost
On this open sunlit road
The colors of your shadow
Mixing with the sky
A seed of hope
In you finally grows
In this glowing atmosphere
You breathe in life

Looking up to hope

Dark shallows

I see a mirror of hope
Burning through you
Prisoner of the stars
And their cold shadows

In the wide awake night
Your feelings come true
You are a beam of life
In the dark shallows

Wrinkles

Wrinkles
On the pathway
Sorrow and tears
Of yesterday
Water the flowers within
My past
Turns into Spring

Sylvia Plath

She was a poet
Bathing in the sky
Lying in silver snow
Moonlight stronger
Than sorrow
Bringing her smile
And words
Back to life

Free

Wild horses hair
She wears with a smile
Life in the air
She walks
With the sunshine
Never afraid to dare

Dare the stars, the darkness
We were broke but
The mesmerizing beauty
Of our wildernesses
Created us

White scars

I like to look high
At the white scars
Left by the airplanes
In the burning
Summer skies
So evanescent
Like the wounds
That mark my body
One day painful
Another vanished

Stars align

You were afraid
Of not seeing
Another tomorrow
Awaking by your side
So I brought you a mirror
Before your last night
Look through those eyes
You see
The stars align
Life flows
In the right direction

Blind hope

Blind, bumping into
The walls of my thoughts
Writing till the blood dries
The ink of my eyes
Heart asleep, but hope
Pure as a rock
Turning words into
An invisible sunrise

Unstoppable

Walking on water
Not dreaming
Walking so fast
The ground turns to light
Tears shooting stars
On your illuminated cheeks
Soon you'll be a sun
Breaking free
Not dreaming
Unstoppable

Drops of hope

Picking up fragments of sky
That fell down into your heart
Like drops of hope
In the middle of the dark
Keep them close to me
Cast in the depths of your soul

Thoughts starside

In your thoughts
By the night stand
What does it cost
To picture yourself
In a land with
No gravity
Holding your feelings down
But letting you fly
For the time
Of a night
Starside

Many thoughts

Asking the stars questions
My heart cannot solve
On a hill to the sky
With evening grass
Under one hand
And too many thoughts
In the hollow
Of the other

Space blues

Shades of blues

Shades of blues
As tears flow by
Drops twinkling on
A glassy night sky
Shooting scars
Marking my mind
Evanescent memories
Make me blind

Ice breaker

You traveled to nights
No one has seen before
And broke through my soul
Like an ice breaker

The fire
Lit within
I can show you
Parts of me
That you can only see
Through
The softest lenses

Sinking ship

Thinking of a time
When stars once drowned
Like a sinking ship
In the black hole
Of my mind
Echoing in
The nothingness

This other side

Every time I look up
I meet your eyes
From a distance
Like this other side
They call love

I drown
In your sky above

Boy blue

Boy blue
From outer space
Down to earth
But in the clouds I guess

Wanderlust at night
Dreamer by day
Blue like the sky

When the stars cry

When the stars cry
By the billion over you
And the night
Shatters into fragments
Of sunrise

All these lights meet
Your deepest blue

Space field of my mind

If you feel
Dark or blue
Like a night
With no colors
Ask for my heart

I would write
Suns to you
From the space field
Of my mind

Satellite heart

Bathing in the echoes
Of your satellite heart
Glowing whispers
Of your soul in the dark

Catch you with my eyes
My hands keep your light
'Cause the music of you
I listen to at night

End of days

Flirting with the gaps
Between your fingers

Just like
The lack of time
We have left together
Before the end
Of days

Shooting star tears

People will remember
Those shooting star tears
You cried so hard
To light up
Other people's lonely nights

A while

The only stars I need
Are from the depths
Of your night eyes
With a smile
Like sunshine
I haven't seen
In a while

Starry hands

If you were the sunrise
And me the night
I would embrace you
With starry hands
On the top of the highest hill

Watch you awaking
Not losing anything
Of your deepest light

Stars and beyond

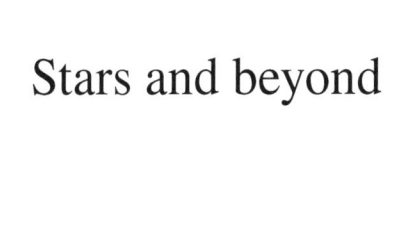

The place I call home

The Moon is the
Only place I call home
For my heart
Belongs with the stars

A quiet paradise
Where I'm all alone
I see dark skies
With luminous scars

Planet of love

Your love is a planet
In singular darkness
That you can't see
With your eyes

But with a mindfulness
Stronger than loneliness
You're my Earth
And I'm your open sky

Front row seat by your heart

If this is my last night
By your side
I will stay up all night
In a front row seat
By your heart
And watch it
Slowly fall asleep
While a galaxy of dreams
Brings unknown colors
To this unique spectacle

The galaxy of your soul

Take me to the forgotten
Galaxy of your soul
Its stars shed a light
Of a beauty
Words can't tell

My mindfulness
In your company
No longer dull
A kaleidoscope
From a heaven
In the middle of a hell

Yellow Mustang star

Drifting through
The dead end
Of the infinite
Lost in space
On my yellow Mustang star
Flirting with nothingness
And touching
My darkest nights
I bring life to this dream
I call interstellar

The planets of your eyes

The planets of your eyes
Hide a secret paradise
Dark constellated oceans
Of dawn and twilight

Contemplating through you
A thousand and one sunrises
From the mountain of your soul
Shades of velvet night

Stars pianist

You sleep in
A roofless bedroom
To better play
Piano notes
With the stars
At the tips
Of your fingers

Sketching galaxies
For others to feel
While looking
Up high

Into the blue

Big wide dive
Into the blue
A sea above
With no stars

I've already
Given them all
To you

Wonder

Butterflies

It is no secret
To the world
That you are heaven
To my eyes

The way you
Say your words
Turns rain drops
Into butterflies

Like a movie

The thunder of your heart
Tearing out our galaxies
Pieces of life and a past
That my eyes can recall

Your smile like a movie
Reflecting in my tears
Dropping like leaves
In the fall

Soft tide

Sunny snow flakes falling
Inside your eyes
Starry reflections
Spreading with grace
Like lightning drowning
In ocean deep skies

Soft tide flowing
Over your sleeping face

Mirror ocean

Walking on a mirror ocean
The surface reflecting
The call of the stars

Lying down and feeling complete
The cracks on this ocean
Hide
The most heavenly parts of me
I didn't think existed

Moon heart

I can see your moon heart
Through my telescope
Scars on it
From a fight f
For hope

If shooting stars were
Arrows in the night
Your scars would be
Valleys filled with light

The shadow of the mountain

The shadow of the mountain
Left me speechless
With stars
Projected onto the screen
Of my contemplating soul

Frozen lake

Your mind is
The most beautiful
Frozen lake
Silver surface with
Moonlight reflections
Closed eyes but never felt
So awake

Like melted lightning
At my feet
In fusion

Rainbow fire

I start a rainbow fire
Within you
So the world can see
What you hide

Flames of unknown colors
Come true
And bloom in a sky
Where night dies

Grow free

Thinking of a time
When the grass was
Still in love
With the sun

Feeling the distance
From the star
That made it
Grow free

Starry face

Night shade
Thrown over
Your starry face
Like velvet blue
Shining in slow motion

With retro lenses
Capturing such grace
The movie theater of my mind
Playing my emotions

Matches

Stars
From the sparks
Of the matches
You asked me to light
In your dark

Contemplation

Sparkles by the million
Racing through us
We go so fast
We can't breathe
Breathtaking
To seek beauty in lights
That transcend our minds
Or just to have tears
Of such contemplation
Rolling down our cheeks

Holding your hand
Through the night
With too many stars
We go so fast
We just can't
Breathe

Many oceans

Many oceans
You have within
But the one and only
I can dive in
Is made of
Your coolest light

Wide alive

Nothing compares
To these waves
Crawling over your face
Under water five seconds
Feels like a million

Seeing stars in the sand
Washed ashore
In slow motion
Above my eyes
Makes me feel once more
Wide alive

Night lights

Naked soul

Unwrapping your soul
In the moonlight
Made of night
And unknown colors

Vanishing from my hands
But still so bright
Like stardust from
Fragments of life

Drum thunder

Loud drum thunder
Illuminating
Your soul
In the dark
Diluted with the echoes
Of your heart
And its sparks

Universe noises and fireworks
In slow motion
Like a moving painting
Mesmerizing emotions

Cup of sun

Awaking to shades of night
In my cup of sun
I bathe in
Waves of light
Washing through me
At midnight

Close your eyes
And breathe in life

Whispers of night

I wake up to lights
And whispers of night
A feeling of day
In the middle of darkness

The echoes of
Your glowing heart
Too bright

Blind, but seeing
The beauty of nothingness

Walking on water

Walking on water
The surface
Is a sky
And the depths
Made of life and night

Each of my steps
Made of the glow
You filled me with
So long ago

Dawn in the eyes

Soft dew pearling down
From your eyes

Shades of dawn
Inside them

That I watch
From the sunrise
To the deep end

River wild

Running down
A river wild
A shadow of you
In the flow

The sparkling sun
I follow
Down this river wild

Evening fog

I met you in an evening fog
Your steps cloud lit
The coolness of light
Flowing onto my night face

These memories lost
With the thickening
Of your clouds

I lost track of your light

Roses of light

Roses of light
Project shadows
Onto your face
Like twinkling petals
Over a deep night veil

The wanderlust I am
Has lost many times its way
In those eyes of yours
Like velvet sunlight

An illusion of day

Blossom voices

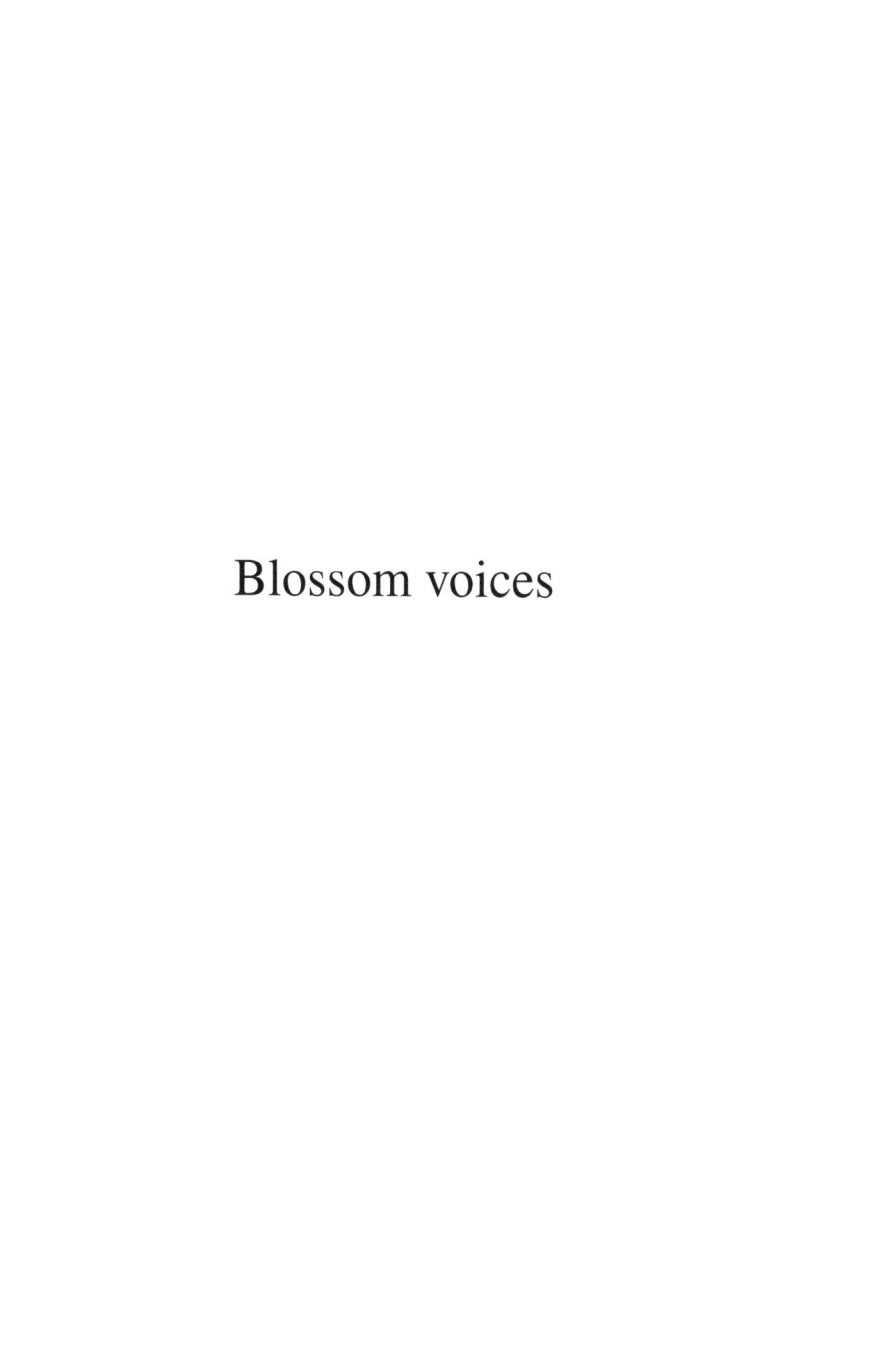

Eyes of yesterday

Flowers flowing
On the riverside
Through the eyes
Of yesterday

Following this voice
Inside
Where colored ghosts
Of roses lie

Bud of magnificence

So I sat
In a void of silence
And my flower found
Its roots
In this quietness

A bud
Of magnificence

Luminous blossoms

Words that heal
Are like luminous blossoms

Those lights
That enlighten
Your steps
Through the field
Of a journey
In the dark

Wilted flower blues

Guessing flower silhouettes
In a velvet night

Feeling with my fingertips
The fragile lights
That once lifted them
From the ground
All the way up
To the sky

Wide moons

Wide moons
Will light the flowers
You gathered

Throw them
Into the sky
And watch them bloom
In the night

Teach flowers to live

You could seed flowers
And teach them
How to reach the sky

Others won't
And take for granted
The beauty they hide

Dandelion

A dandelion mind
Tends to dream
Not only at night
And escapes from reality
In the simplicity
Of the invisible breeze
And soft daylight

Dream away their nights

Do the roses
Have the blues
When they
Miss the sunny wind
That makes them
Feel alive?

They might still have
The warmth of
Distant stars
To dream away
Their nights

Words for oneself

Flowers torn alive

If humans have always
Sought destruction

Is it for some deep reason
Or the desire
To break forever
The innocence
Of flowers, torn alive

Just for the beauty
Of that image

To fall in love

To fall in love
Means that
Your soul is
Too heavy
To follow
The lightness
Of your heart
When you feel
Struck by
Lightning
Of your own

Happiness

Happiness isn't something
You pick up at your feet
It's a mountain you climb
For once at its summit
You wonder:

Look at who I am
See what I have
Been through

Gravity

When gravity holds
Your heavy soul
To the ground
Remember:

Flowers rise and bloom
After the coldest winter

The void between stars

They say that
Gaps between fingers
Are made to be filled
By someone else's

What if the void between stars
Was made to have
Enough space
To wander off

Blind wanderer

Where does
The blind wanderer
Lay his head down to dream
When stars and nights
Are made of nothingness

Maybe in a place
Most of us
Can't even picture
The colors of

Move on

Shooting stars
Travel through
The darkest depths
But go on shining
For themselves

So why wouldn't you
Try to do so
As well
And move on

Field of tomorrow

It takes courage
To let it go
To better bloom
In the field
Of an unknown
Tomorrow

Dreams echo within

Like a pillow
That takes the shape
Of our sleeping heads
At night
Our dreams
Echo within
And push back
The boundaries
We set ourselves
During the day

Like a tree

Like a tree
I wish I knew
How to stay still
Rooted beautifully
My arms
Stretching to the sky
Like branches

Whatever the weather
Whatever the season
My wrinkled bark
Keeping me strong

Atoms

Being made of atoms
The dust of stars
Means that
You are
The whole universe
Itself
So
Do not denigrate
Yourself
When you feel small
Or like nothing at all

Treasure within

Sometimes
The greatest treasure
Isn't made of gold
Nor any precious stones
But of something within

A simple flame
You manage with courage
To keep alive
Despite the storms

Above all

Strength
Isn't about
Moving mountains
To the stars
And beyond
If you can

It's above all
Staying rooted
When those stars
You wished upon before
Shatter over you

Look up to life

You cast your fears
Up into sunny altitudes
For once they're gone
You are not afraid
To look up to life
And kiss the sky back
Again

Contents

Preface 5

Lost in between

Glowing heart	11
Mermaid	12
Seabed of your ocean	13
The eyes of dew	14
My compass	15
Is it you	16
Inner stars	17
Open sunlit road	18

Looking up to hope

Dark shallows	23
Wrinkles	24
Sylvia Plath	25
Free	26
White scars	27
Stars align	28

Blind hope	29
Unstoppable	30
Drops of hope	31
Thoughts starside	32
Many thoughts	33

Space blues

Shades of blues	37
Ice breaker	38
Sinking ship	39
This other side	40
Boy blue	41
When the stars cry	42
Space field of my mind	43
Satellite heart	44
End of days	45
Shooting star tears	46
A while	47
Starry hands	48

Stars and beyond

The place I call home	53
Planet of love	54
Front row seat by your heart	55
The galaxy of your soul	56
Yellow Mustang star	57
The planets of your eyes	58
Stars pianist	59
Into the blue	60

Wonder

Butterflies	65
Like a movie	66
Soft tide	67
Mirror ocean	68
Moon heart	69
The shadow of the mountain	70
Frozen lake	71
Rainbow fire	72
Grow free	73
Starry face	74

Matches	75
Contemplation	76
Many oceans	77
Wide alive	78

Night lights

Naked soul	83
Drum thunder	84
Cup of sun	85
Whispers of night	86
Walking on water	87
Dawn in the eyes	88
River wild	89
Evening fog	90
Roses of light	91

Blossom voices

Eyes of yesterday	95
Bud of magnificence	96
Luminous blossoms	97
Wilted flower blues	98
Wide moons	99
Teach flowers to live	100
Dandelion	101
Dream away their nights	102

Words for oneself

Flowers torn alive	107
To fall in love	108
Happiness	109
Gravity	110
The void between stars	111
Blind wanderer	112
Move on	113
Field of tomorrow	114
Dreams echo within	115
Like a tree	116

Atoms	117
Treasure within	118
Above all	119
Look up to life	120

Instagram : @willi_ame98

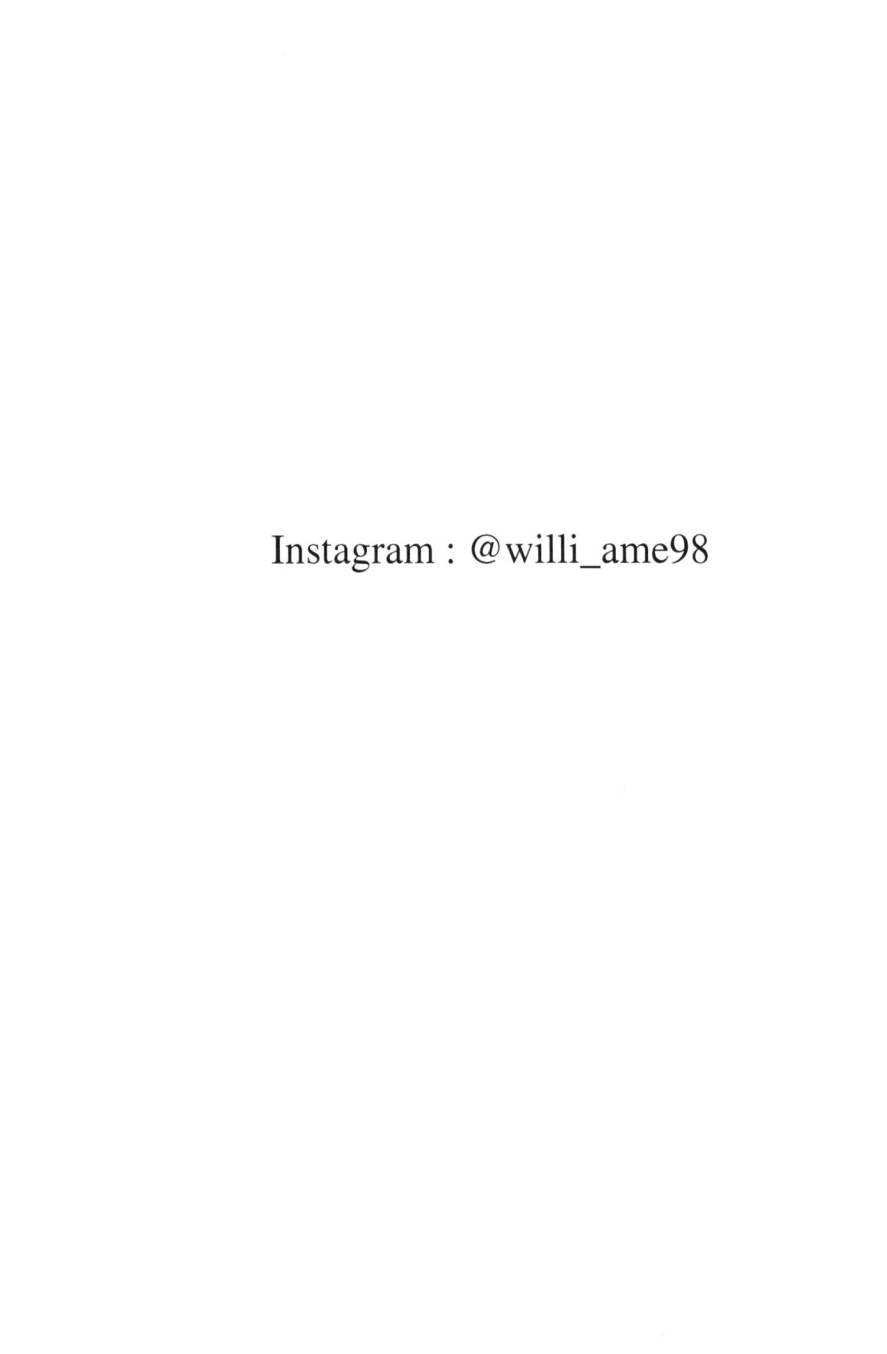

Printed in Great Britain
by Amazon

40412169R10075